Five-Minute Devotions

for Children

CELEBRATING GOD'S WORLD AS A FAMILY

Written by Pamela Kennedy
Illustrated by Amy Wummer

ideals children's books™
Nashville, Tennessee

ISBN-13: 978-0-8249-5485-7
ISBN-10: 0-8249-5485-8

Published by Ideals Children's Books
An imprint of Ideals Publications
A Guideposts Company
Nashville, Tennessee
www.idealsbooks.com

Color separations by Precision Color Graphics, Franklin, Wisconsin

Printed and bound in Italy

Library of Congress Cataloging-in-Publication Data

Kennedy, Pamela, date.
  Five minute devotions for children : celebrating God's world as a family
/ written by Pamela Kennedy ; illustrated by Amy Wummer.
      p. cm.
  ISBN-13: 978-0-8249-5485-7
  ISBN-10: 0-8249-5485-8 (alk. paper)
  1. Children—Prayer-books and devotions—English. 2. Family—Religious
life. I. Wummer, Amy. II. Title.
  BV4870.K466 2004
  242'.62—dc22
                                 2004004030

Designed by Eve DeGrie

For Josh, Doug, and Anne, who taught me
to look at the world through the eyes of a child. –P.J.K.

In loving memory of my dad, Spin. –A.W.

Lego_Aug10_10

Contents

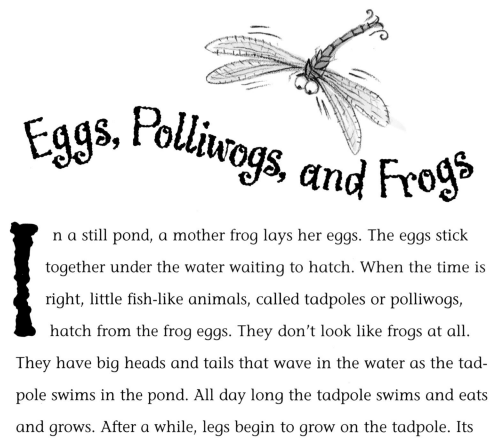

Eggs, Polliwogs, and Frogs

In a still pond, a mother frog lays her eggs. The eggs stick together under the water waiting to hatch. When the time is right, little fish-like animals, called tadpoles or polliwogs, hatch from the frog eggs. They don't look like frogs at all. They have big heads and tails that wave in the water as the tadpole swims in the pond. All day long the tadpole swims and eats and grows. After a while, legs begin to grow on the tadpole. Its body gets longer and its gills begin to disappear. After more time has passed, the tadpole begins to grow front legs and its tail begins to disappear. It looks more like a frog and is called a froglet. Finally, the tail is gone and the frog is all grown up. It breathes air, but it can still swim when it wants to.

God makes all things grow and change. Just like the polliwog, you will get bigger and grow stronger. One day you may even be as tall as your Daddy or Mommy. Every day you are learning new things. God has wonderful plans for you as you grow up.

What do you say?

• Can you find the frog eggs in the picture?

• What is another name for the tadpole?

• What is something you might like to do when you grow up?

• Why do you think God makes all things grow and change?

What does God say?

So Jesus grew both in height and in wisdom, and he was loved by God and by all who knew him.

LUKE 2:52

7

Ants, Ants, Ants

Maybe you have seen ants walking on the sidewalk or in the grass—or even in your house. Ants are small, but they are very strong. They can carry something that weighs five times more than they do. Ants spend most of their time working to gather food and taking care of their nest. When a job is too hard for one ant to do, it will go get some other ants to help. Ants don't talk like people, but they can share messages by touching their antennae together and by leaving trails for other ants to smell. When the ants work together, they can carry big things that are too heavy for one ant to carry alone.

Sometimes you may feel small, but you can do work too. You can help at home and at school. When there is a lot of work to do, you might need to ask for help or help someone else just like the ant. It makes God happy when we work together and help each other to do our best.

What do you say?

• What kinds of things are the ants in the picture carrying?

• How much can one ant carry?

• What is a job you can do to help at home or at school?

• Why do you think God wants us to work together?

What does God say?

Take a lesson from the ants, you lazybones. Learn from their ways and be wise!

PROVERBS 6:6

Disappearing Tails

Geckos are the only lizards that make sounds other than hissing. The noise they make is a clicking that almost sounds like their name: *Geck-o*. Geckos have sticky toe pads that allow them to climb straight up walls and even across ceilings. Geckos have another unusual trait. When a person or animal catches a gecko by the tail, the little lizard drops its tail and runs away. Losing a tail doesn't even hurt the gecko, in fact, it can grow a new one in a few weeks! God has given the gecko a wonderful way to escape from an enemy and keep from getting hurt.

When we are being hurt or are frightened, it is sometimes a good thing to run to a safe place. We cannot leave a part of ourselves behind, but God has given us a way to be safe too. We can tell a grown up that we trust and ask them to help us. We can ask God to help us too. God wants all of his creation to be safe.

10

What do you say?

• Can you count the geckos in this picture?

• What can the gecko do when he is caught or frightened?

• What is something that frightens you? Where could you go to be safe?

• Why do you think God wants all of his creation to be safe?

What does God say?

The name of the LORD is a strong fortress; the godly run to him and are safe.
PROVERBS 18:10

11

Playful Sea Otters

The sea otter spends almost all of its life in the water. Otters love to dive and splash and swim from morning to night. The otter's favorite foods are abalone and sea urchins. These both have hard shells, but the clever little otter has figured out a way to crack them open. The otter finds a stone or smooth rock, tucks it under its front leg, scoops up an abalone or urchin, and then back-floats on the surface of the water with the stone resting on its tummy. Grabbing the shellfish, the otter smacks it against the stone until it cracks. Then he eats the juicy meat inside the shell. After all this hard work, the otter is tired. He makes his bed in the water too. The otter rolls up in a long piece of seaweed then falls asleep, cozy in the kelp blanket while the soft waves rock him to sleep.

Just like sea otters, children love to play all day. After running and jumping and climbing they get tired too. God knows that all animals and people need to rest. He wants us to get sleep so we can be healthy and happy. When we sleep, our bodies grow and get stronger. Playing and resting are both important.

What do you say?

• Can you find the sleeping otter in the picture?

• How do otters open the shellfish that they love to eat?

• Where is your favorite place to sleep? What kinds of things do you sleep with?

• Why do you think God wants all of his creation to rest?

What does God say?

I will lie down in peace and sleep, for you alone, O LORD, will keep me safe.
PSALM 4:8

13

Deep Water Friends

Dolphins are small members of the whale family. Although they swim in the oceans, they breathe air through a special opening in the tops of their heads. They must come to the surface often to take a breath. They usually swim with several other dolphins and leap and dive together in the ocean's waves. Sometimes they even ride the waves like a surfer does! But dolphins also care for one another in a very special way. If one dolphin is hurt, its friends will stay close to it and protect it from harm. They may even push the sick dolphin to the surface, so it can take a breath. If its friends didn't help out, the sick dolphin might drown.

God has given each of us good friends to play with and to help. We all know how wonderful it is to have a good friend when we are feeling lonely, hurt, or sad. God wants us to be good friends to others too. When someone is alone, we can ask him or her to play with us. When someone is sad, we can share a hug or just listen if they want to tell us what is wrong. Good friends are a special gift from God.

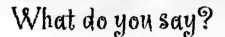

What do you say?

- Can you find the place on their heads where the dolphins breathe?

- How has a friend helped you? What could you do to help a friend?

- How do the dolphins help one another?

- Why do you think God wants us to be good friends to one another?

What does God say?

A friend is always loyal, and a brother is born to help in time of need.

PROVERBS 17:17

15

A Selfish Bird

Have you ever seen a cuckoo clock? These clocks look like little houses, and near the peak of the roof there is a door. At the hour and half-hour, the door opens and a little toy bird pops out and says, "Cuckoo!" The little bird in the clock is very helpful, but the real bird that the clock is named after is not a very helpful bird at all. The cuckoo is a bird that seems very selfish. When a mother cuckoo wants to lay her egg, she doesn't build her own nest. Instead, she looks for the nest of another bird. Then she lays her egg in that nest and flies away. When the baby cuckoo hatches, it usually shoves all the other eggs out of the nest. Then the cuckoo chick gets all the food and all the attention from its new mother. The cuckoo doesn't care about anyone but itself.

Some children act just like the cuckoo. They take things that aren't theirs, and they want all the attention they can get. When they act this way, others don't enjoy being their friends. God wants us to be happy, and he knows that we are much happier when we share with others and treat them with kindness.

What do you say?

- Can you find the cuckoo?

- What does the cuckoo do to the other birds that live around it?

- What are some things you could do to show that you are not selfish?

- Why do you think God wants his children to share with others and be kind?

What does God say?

Don't forget to do good and to share what you have with those in need, for such sacrifices are very pleasing to God.
HEBREWS 13:16

17

Patient Penguins

Emperor penguins live in Antarctica and are the largest of all the penguins. They swim in the water most of the time; but during the winter, they come up onto the thick ice. There each mother penguin lays one big egg. Because the egg will freeze if it is left on the ice, the mother rolls it on top of the father penguin's feet. He balances the egg there very carefully and covers it with a thick fold of skin to keep it warm. The father penguin huddles on the ice together with the other fathers and keeps his egg warm for about fifty-four days. All this time he does not eat. He gets thinner and thinner, but he waits patiently for the baby penguin to hatch. No matter how cold or hungry he gets, the father penguin doesn't leave the egg. When the egg finally hatches, the mother returns to help care for the baby and the father can get some food.

Just like the father penguin, sometimes we must be patient and wait for things too. Waiting can seem very hard, especially when we are tired or hungry. But God reminds us that when we are patient, we are showing love. God blesses us when we wait patiently.

What do you say?

• Can you find the eggs that the father penguins are keeping warm?

• What is something you could wait for patiently like the penguin?

• How does the father penguin show that he is being patient?

• Why do you think God says love is patient?

What does God say?

Love is patient and kind.
1 CORINTHIANS 13:4A

19

School for Bears

Grizzly bears are known for being large and very ferocious. They can be up to seven feet tall and weigh over five hundred pounds. But when grizzly cubs are born, they are very small and helpless. A newborn cub is blind and has no teeth and no fur. It is only eight inches long and weighs just over a pound. It's about the size of a big banana! But cubs grow fast. By the time the grizzly cub is a few months old, its mother is already teaching it many things. She shows her cubs how to find berries, roots, and nuts. She also teaches the cubs how to catch fish. Grizzlies like to stand beside a stream and scoop salmon out of the water with their big paws. The little cubs must practice many times before they catch their first fish. The mother teaches them to hunt, fish, and to protect themselves from danger. They learn new things every day.

Just like bear cubs, people need to learn many things too. Our parents and teachers help us learn to read, to ride a bike, to tie our shoes, to dance, to play a musical instrument, and to understand about God and the Bible. Learning is fun and exciting and helps everyone grow.

What do you say?

• What do you think the cubs in the picture are learning?

• What do grizzly cubs look like when they are born?

• Name something you are learning to do.

• Why do you think God wants people to learn about him?

What does God say?

*[Jesus said] . . .
Let me teach you,
because I am humble
and gentle, and you will
find rest for your souls.*
MATTHEW 11:29

21

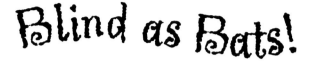

Blind as Bats!

Many people say that a person who cannot find something is "as blind as a bat." Bats, however, have perfectly good eyes and can see fine in the daytime. But during the day, bats usually sleep hanging upside down by their feet. When night comes, bats leave their nesting areas or roosts and fly in search of their favorite food, juicy insects. Because it is dark at night, bats cannot use their eyes to find flying insects so they use their ears instead. Bats make rapid, high-pitched squeaks. These squeaks echo off insects and bounce back to the bat's very sensitive ears. By listening very carefully, the bat knows just where the insect is and can either catch it in its mouth or scoop it up with one of its webbed wings. By using its ears the bat can find all it needs to survive.

People have ears that are not as sensitive as a bat's, but we need to listen too. God has given us ears to hear many things. We listen to words that teach us and warn us of danger. We hear beautiful music and funny stories. Our ears help us learn about God and his plans for us. Listening carefully is an important way to learn and grow.

What do you say?

• Look at the picture. Which bat is about to catch its dinner?

• What are some of your favorite sounds?

• How do bats "see" with their ears?

• Why do you think God wants his children to be good listeners?

What does God say?

My dear brothers and sisters, be quick to listen, slow to speak, and slow to get angry.
JAMES 1:19

23

Watch Out for Wildcats!

Wildcats look very much like pet cats called tabbies. Their coats are marked with brown and tan stripes, and they have golden or green eyes. They look friendly; but if you ever meet one, look out! Wildcats are very dangerous and powerful. They become fierce fighters if they think another animal or a person is trespassing on their territory. They snarl, flatten their ears, arch their backs, and curl back their lips to show their long, sharp teeth. They will attack, scratching and biting, if they feel threatened or afraid. When a wildcat is angry, it is a good thing to stay far away!

Some people are like wildcats. They seem to be friendly; but when they become angry, they say and do things that are hurtful. God wants his children to be kind to one another and to control their anger. When we are angry we need to talk about how we feel instead of punching or hitting other people or calling them names. We can even tell God about being angry and ask him to help us control ourselves. Everyone gets angry sometimes, but no one should act like a wildcat!

What do you say?

• How can you tell that the wildcat in the picture is angry?

• What makes you angry? How do you act when you are angry?

• Why are wildcats dangerous?

• Why do you think God wants us to control ourselves when we are angry?

What does God say?

And don't sin by letting anger gain control over you. Don't let the sun go down while you are still angry, for anger gives a mighty foothold to the Devil.
EPHESIANS 4:26-27

25

Gorilla Families

Gorillas are the largest members of the ape family. They live in the mountains and lowlands of Africa. Although there are movies and stories about fierce, giant gorillas, most gorillas live quiet and peaceful lives in small family groups. Both father and mother gorillas help care for their children. They are patient teachers and spend many hours playing games with their babies. When little gorillas are tired or frightened, their parents will pick them up and hug them or carry them on their backs. Mother gorillas teach their children how to build sleeping nests and how to find good things to eat. Young gorillas enjoy climbing and wrestling just like human children.

God has placed people in families too. People in families protect and love one another. Just like the gorillas, we can learn many things in our families. We learn to work and play together, to respect one another, and to do our part to help the family. God says that he is like a father to all his children. In a very special way, everyone who loves God belongs to his family; and it pleases God when we love all our brothers and sisters.

What do you say?

• How many baby gorillas can you find in the picture?

• How many people are in your family? Can you name them all?

• What kinds of things do gorillas do in their families?

• Why do you think God places people in families?

What does God say?

Whenever we have the opportunity, we should do good to everyone, especially to our Christian brothers and sisters.
GALATIANS 6:10

27

Scary Owls

Barn owls are sometimes called the "ghosts of the barn-yard." They aren't ghosts at all, but large, white and tan birds that help farmers get rid of pests like rats and mice. The reason people have made up scary stories about barn owls is because when they fly at night, hunting for food, their light feathers seem to glow in the dark. The owls also make spooky sounds like screeches, wails, and hissing. They swoop over fields and meadows just a few feet above the ground and sometimes startle people who might be outside for a walk. Farmers know that owls are their friends and often make special places in their barns where the owls can make their nests.

God knows that when we don't understand things, we often become frightened, especially at night when it is dark. Sometimes we make up scary stories to explain these things. Then we get even more scared! In the Bible, God tells us that he loves us and that we can trust him. He knows that there are many things we don't understand, but he doesn't want us to be afraid. God is with us in the daytime as well as in the night.

What do you say?

• In the picture, can you find the owl that is nesting and the two owls that are hunting?

• Why have people made up scary stories about the barn owl?

• How can trusting God help us when we are afraid?

• What are some things that make you afraid?

What does God say?

But when I am afraid, I put my trust in you.
Psalm 56:3

29

Busy Beavers

The beaver is an animal that works very hard. Beavers build their homes, or dams, in streams and ponds. When a beaver wants to build a dam, it waddles on its short legs to find a small tree. Then the beaver begins gnawing at the tree trunk with its long, sharp front teeth. In just a few minutes, a busy beaver can cut down a trunk that is five inches thick. Then the beaver trims off the small branches, cuts the trunk in shorter lengths, and drags the heavy limbs back to the building site. Carefully, the beaver weaves sticks, branches, reeds, and small tree trunks together, then fills in the spaces with mud to make its dam secure. Even a good dam gets damaged, so the beaver must constantly be on the watch to repair holes caused by weather or other animals. Beavers never quit working. If they did, their homes might break apart and float away!

Just like the busy beaver, we sometimes have jobs that take time to finish. If we quit when we get tired or bored, the job will not get done. The Bible calls working hard and not giving up, *endurance*. If we have endurance, we will finish what we begin. We can be proud about doing good work, just like the busy beaver!

What do you say?

- Look at the picture. How many trees have these busy beavers cut down?

- How does a beaver build a new dam?

- What kind of work is hard for you to finish?

- Why do you think God wants us to have endurance?

What does God say?

. . . for when your endurance is fully developed, you will be strong in character and ready for anything.

James 1:4

31

Rattlesnake Warnings

The rattlesnake is a large desert reptile with a bad reputation. Usually the snake stays away from people; but if someone comes near the rattler, it will hold its tail upright and shake the end. There are several hollow rattles on the end of the snake's tail made of material just like your fingernails. When the snake shakes these, they make a buzzing sound that means, "Danger! Stay Away!" If the rattler's warning is ignored, the snake will strike out and bite with poisonous fangs. The poison can make a person very sick. Some people even die from rattlesnake bites. If you ever hear a rattlesnake's warning, be sure to get away fast!

God doesn't want us to be hurt because we do not know about danger. That is why he gives us many warnings in the Bible. Just like the rattle of the rattlesnake, God's warnings tell us to stay away from things that are harmful. He tells us to stay away from lying, from stealing, from being selfish, and from being mean to others. If we follow God's warnings, we will be happier and safer. God warns us of these dangers because he loves us.

What do you say?

• Which rattlesnake in the picture is sending a message that says "Danger!"

• How can you know if a rattlesnake is getting ready to bite?

• What are some dangerous things you have been warned about?

• Why do you think God wants us to follow his warnings?

What does God say?

A prudent person foresees the danger ahead and takes precautions; the simpleton goes blindly on and suffers the consequences.

PROVERBS 22:3

33

Singing Whales

Many people think that birds are the best singers in the animal kingdom, but do you know what kind of animal sings the longest and most complicated kinds of songs? It's not a tiny bird, but a thirty-ton humpback whale! These huge sea creatures are longer than a school bus and the songs they sing can be heard underwater for twenty miles! Scientists have listened to whale songs with special microphones and have discovered that a group of male whales located in the same area will often all sing the same song at the same time. The whale songs contain moans, clicks, chirps, creaks, and groans. Sometimes the songs last for ten or fifteen minutes! No one knows exactly why the whales sing. They could be happy or upset or even in love.

Just like the humpback whales, people like to sing too. The Bible tells us that God loves to hear his children sing and make music. Whether our songs are happy or sad, we can enjoy singing them. Making up songs is a great way to share our feelings and even to tell God how much we love him.

What do you say?

• What kind of animal sings the longest songs?

• Why do you think the humpback whales sing?

• What kinds of songs do you like best? Can you sing your favorite song?

• Why do you think God likes to hear his children sing?

What does God say?

I will sing to the LORD because he has been so good to me.
PSALM 13:6

Strange Friends

In the grasslands of southern Africa are two strange friends. One is the redbilled oxpecker, a brown and yellow bird with a bright red bill. Its best friend is the rhinoceros! If you look closely at rhinos you will often see oxpeckers riding along on their backs or climbing on their heads. The rhino likes to give the little bird a ride, because the oxpecker keeps the huge animal healthy and clean by eating pesky flies, ticks, fleas, and dead skin. Another way the bird helps the rhino is by making a sharp call when it sees danger. This helps the rhino because he doesn't see very well. The oxpecker and the rhino may seem like strange friends, but they help one another every day.

Just like the bird and the rhino, people need friends too. God knows that we would be lonely without friends. Friends help one another in many ways. We listen to each other, play together, work together, and share what we have. The Bible teaches us to treat our friends the way we would like to be treated.

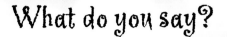

What do you say?

• Can you find all the oxpeckers in the picture?

• How do the oxpecker and the rhino help each other?

• What are some of the things you do to help your friends?

• Why do you think God wants us to be good friends to each other?

What does God say?

Do for others what you would like them to do for you.
MATTHEW 7:12A

Talented Aardvarks

The aardvark is an odd-looking animal that spends its days sleeping and its nights hunting for its favorite food—ants! This shy animal is especially suited for hunting these insects. It has large ears, able to listen for danger, and a sensitive nose that can sniff out any signs of an anthill. The aardvark runs along close to the ground on short legs, and when it finds an insect nest, the hungry aardvark quickly digs into it with powerful front feet and strong claws. When the nest is opened, the aardvark sticks its snout into the hole and searches for ants with its long, sticky tongue. The aardvark can close its nostrils so insects can't run up its nose, and its thick skin protects it from the bites of the angry ants. Even though the aardvark is a timid animal, it has everything it needs to be a great ant hunter.

Just like the aardvark, you have been given special gifts and abilities by God too. Perhaps you can run fast or read well. Maybe you can do math problems with ease or sing and dance. You might be especially good at making others happy or doing kind things. God knows each one of his children and he has given each of us exactly what we need to succeed.

What do you say?

- What is the aardvark doing in the picture?

- What are some things you can do well?

- What are some of the things that make the aardvark such a good ant hunter?

- Why do you think God gives each of us special talents and abilities?

What does God say?

God has given each of us the ability to do certain things well.
ROMANS 12:6A

Angry Hippos

If you looked at a hippopotamus yawning in a slow-moving African river, you might think it is a friendly and lazy animal. But you would be mistaken! Armed with long, razor-sharp teeth, the hippo is actually one of the most dangerous African animals. What makes it so dangerous is its temper. If a boat comes too close, the hippopotamus will lunge out with a loud roar and slash at it. The boat may be overturned and any riders bitten or dragged under water and drowned. When hippos fight with one another, they may battle for an hour or more, leaving each other gashed and bleeding! These animals may look peaceful, but don't make them mad!

Sometimes people can have nasty tempers just like the hippo. They are just fine until someone bothers them. Then they use angry words or even fists to fight. They hurt other people and lose friends. No one likes to be around someone who gets mad and always wants to fight. God tells us to be friends and to settle our differences peacefully. He knows that when we lose our tempers, we hurt others and ourselves too.

What do you say?

• Where does the hippo live?

• What makes the hippo such a dangerous animal?

• What kinds of things make you angry? What can you do with your angry feelings so that you don't hurt others?

• Why do you think God wants us to control our tempers?

What does God say?

A fool gives full vent to anger, but a wise person quietly holds it back.

PROVERBS 29:11

41

Caught in a Web

The big, black and yellow garden spider finds a place to spin her orb-shaped web. She uses six tiny spinnerets located under her abdomen to produce different kinds of thin spider silk. Some of the strands are used to anchor the web and others are coated with sticky droplets intended to trap unsuspecting insects. When the garden spider has finished building her web, she sits quietly in the center, waiting for a careless insect to fly into her sticky trap. As soon as one does, the spider rushes to it, bites it to paralyze it, and wraps it in a coating of spider silk. She will eat the dead insect later. As soon as she finishes wrapping up her dinner, the spider hurries back to the center of her web to wait for another insect to come along. She has made a perfect trap!

Lies are a lot like spider webs. They trap the people who tell them. When we tell lies, we feel caught just like the careless insect in the spider's web. But we don't have to worry about being caught in a lie. We can choose to be truthful instead. Telling the truth is the best way to stay out of the web of lies.

What do you say?

• What happens when an insect is caught in a spider's web?

• What is caught in the garden spider's web?

• What happens when we tell lies?

• Why do you think God wants his children to tell the truth?

What does God say?

Then watch your tongue! Keep your lips from telling lies!

PSALM 34:13

43

Prickly Porcupines

The porcupine lives in the woods of North America. Some people have given this animal the nickname "pricklepig" because of its prickly spines. The porcupine has about three hundred thousand sharp quills covering its back, sides, and tail. When another animal comes too close, the porcupine makes its quills stand up. It looks like a giant pincushion! As soon as the curious animal tries to sniff or bite the porcupine, it gets a nose or mouthful of pain. Other animals soon learn to leave the prickly porcupine alone.

Have you ever known people who are like prickly porcupines? Whenever someone new comes along, they act unfriendly and pretty soon the new friend goes away. If we want to have friends, we need to be kind to people and talk with them. We can ask them questions, share our toys, and invite them to play with us. It pleases God when we are kind to others. When we are friendly to people, they will want to be friends with us. It's no fun being a lonely, prickly porcupine!

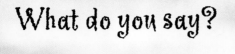

What do you say?

• What animal may get an unhappy surprise from the porcupine?

• Why does the porcupine have the nickname "pricklepig?"

• What can you do to be a friend to someone new?

• Why do you think God asks us to be kind to others?

45

Monkey Business

Spider monkeys live in the rain forests of Central and South America. They are some of the most acrobatic monkeys in the world. With their long arms and legs and their gripping tails, they can swing through the trees with speed and jump from branch to branch without falling. But when spider monkeys are young, they are not very graceful at all. They have to learn how to swing through the trees. Sometimes their mothers help them; but at other times, the young monkeys practice swinging from branch to branch by themselves. Sometimes they slip and fall. Then they must climb back up and try again. It takes lots of practice before they can travel through the trees as well as their parents.

Have you ever tried to do something that your older brother or sister or your parents can do? At first did it seem hard? When we are learning to do new things, we all make mistakes. Just like the spider monkey, we have to try over and over again until we get it right. Practice is a good way to get better at doing things. When you practice riding a bike, singing a song, spelling a word, or reading a book, you get better each time. Don't be afraid to practice—it's the only way to improve!

What do you say?

- How many spider monkeys do you see in the picture?

- What is something you have to practice?

- Why do the spider monkeys have to practice?

- Why do you think God wants us to keep learning new things?

What does God say?

Teach the wise and they will be wiser. Teach the righteous, and they will learn more.

PROVERBS 9:9

47

Pamela Kennedy has written books for all ages of children. When not at the computer, Kennedy teaches part-time at a high school for girls and speaks at Christian retreats and conferences. Pam lives in Honolulu with her husband and their crooked-tailed cat.

Amy Wummer has been illustrating children's books for ten years. Her playful watercolor illustrations for *Five-Minute Devotions* evoke the wonder of a child's delight in the world. She lives in Pennsylvania with her husband, also an artist, and their three children.